CHRISTMAS FOLK

CHRISTMAS FOLK

BY NATALIA BELTING

ILLUSTRATED BY BARBARA COONEY

HOLT, RINEHART AND WINSTON   New York Chicago San Francisco

Books for Young People by Natalia Belting

CHRISTMAS FOLK

WINTER'S EVE

THE STARS ARE SILVER REINDEER

THE EARTH IS ON A FISH'S BACK

CALENDAR MOON

THE SUN IS A GOLDEN EARRING

ELVES AND ELLEFOLK: Tales of Little People

INDY AND MR. LINCOLN

VERITY MULLENS AND THE INDIAN

CAT TALES

Text Copyright © 1969 by Natalia Belting.
Illustrations Copyright © 1969 by Racoon Books.
All rights reserved, including the right to reproduce
this book or portions thereof in any form.
Published simultaneously in Canada by Holt, Rinehart
and Winston of Canada, Limited.
SBN: 03-072375-2 (Trade)
SBN: 03-072380-9 (HLE)
Library of Congress Catalog Card Number: 68-18488
Printed in the United States of America
First Edition

Especially for Christine Clayton

The hallow days of Yule are here.
The nights are long and dark.
A feeble sun scarce warms the day,
And cold congeals the stoutest heart.
    The hallow days of Yule are come,
    And now the Christmas folk bestir,

    And laughter rings, with song,
    And peal of bells,

And spiced smoke from hearths below
Wraps chimney pot and gable cock.

St. Andrew, King,

    Three weeks and three days 'til

    Christmas comes in . . .

The season's begun, the season's come.

For masking and mumming, the season's begun:

    Jack tires himself in granny's gown,

    Jen draws on her gran'ther's breeches.

    Beards of rope,

    Hair of straw,

    Masks of black cloth,

    Or chimney soot.

On the feast of St. Andrew
The mummers go out.

In the dark streets
Ahead of the dawn,
The fiddler comes
And asks
  If we be up.

He fiddles an ancient tune . . .
  "Hunt's up! Hunt's up!"
He fiddles an old, old tune,
Hunsupping at our door.

He calls us each by name.
Bids us rise,
Greet the Yules,
Cry "Joy, joy!"

To Barbara saint all cry full fast
Whose work is in some dangerous craft,
And make full merry,
For 'tis Yule.

Pinwheels stir the evening dusk
In scarlet rounds of fire.

Blue green crystal-bursts
From candle stars
Drop through black
To cobbled lanes.

While all space about
Is roiled by cannon shot.

December 6

Nicolas, good saint of Yule
Dowers poor maids,
Frees boys from school.

Nicolas day
Scholars bar the master out
Until he says,
This Nicolas day,
No school keeps.

On Nicolas day
The mummers go out
　　Guised in masks,
　　With pipes and drums,
　　With fiddles and fifes.
And Robin Hood comes,
Little John, Friar Tuck
Maid Marian,
　　　　The lot of them come.

On Nicolas day,

All come out:

Snap the Dragon,

Hobby the Horse,

and the Christmas Bull.

They all parade,

And every child feasts

At the children's feast,

At the end of Nicolas day.

December 12

      St. Finan's eve,
      The rain is wine,
      The stones are cheese.

In the dark, small boys sit
On the doorstep, tasting the rain.

In the dark, small girls
Try slicing stones
To taste the cheese.

On any, or all of the days of Yule
The mummers go out,
   Guised as St. George, Old Bess, the Fool.
   Garbed as a gypsy, a Spaniard, a Moor.
      Ribboned and gaitered,
      Hid 'neath
         Sheepskins or hides,
      Skirted in straw.

On any or all of the days of Yule,
In the back ways,
In the thick shade,
   Lurk
      Snap the Dragon,
             Hobby the Horse,
                 and the Christmas Bull.

December 17

On Tul-ya-e'en
Trows be seen.

The Green men
And the wee Gray men,
   Are up from under ground,
   Hopping round in dance,
   Riding through the air,
     Astride bulrushes.

In the Yule dusk
Lucky folk
See
   The white pig scamper
     In her red bonnet,
     In her red shoes.

The rest of the folk
See
   Naught
      But a wing of winter mist,
      Twilight-streaked.

December 20

On Thomas' eve no work be done,
Or feast or frolic, none.

> *Ta shape or shu*
> *Ta bake or brew,*
> *Ta reel a prim*
> *Or wind a clew,*
> *A lu soolpaltie*
> *Will tak you.*

But maids will peel
And sleep on onions,
Praying:

> Good St. Thomas, do me right,
> Send me my true love tonight;
> In his clothes and his array,
> Which he weareth every day,
> That I may see him in the face.

December 21

St. Thomas gray, St. Thomas gray,
The longest night and the shortest day.

Thomas' day
The mummers go out:
  Poor folk and old folk,
  Small folk,
All of them girl folk,
And womenfolk,

    In masks and without,
    With gossiping pot and basket and bag
    They trudge from door to door,
    Singing:

        Well a day, well a day
        St. Thomas goes too soon away,
        Then for your gooding we do pray,
        For a good time will not stay.

Wissal, wassail through the town,

If you've got any apples, throw them down.

If you've got no apples, money will do.

 The jug is white and the ale is brown

 And this is the best house in the town.

On Thomas' day,

On any day

 of Yule,

  Mummers go out,

  And with them go

   Snap the Dragon,

    Hobby the Horse,

     and the Christmas Bull.

December 24

The bannocks bake.
The ash log glows.
The Christmas pie cools.
    And round through the town,
    Up and down,
    The Christmas folk go.
        Pitch-dipped brooms,
        Upended, blaze.
                Hills, all heights,
                Like stars,
                Flame fire.

Deep in the mines,
Dark in the caves,
    King Cole calls
    For his fiddlers:
        Their ancient reels
            Swirl up through the mist,
            Whirl through the clamor, the clatter, the echoing peals,
            Twirl, in a giddy-go-round.

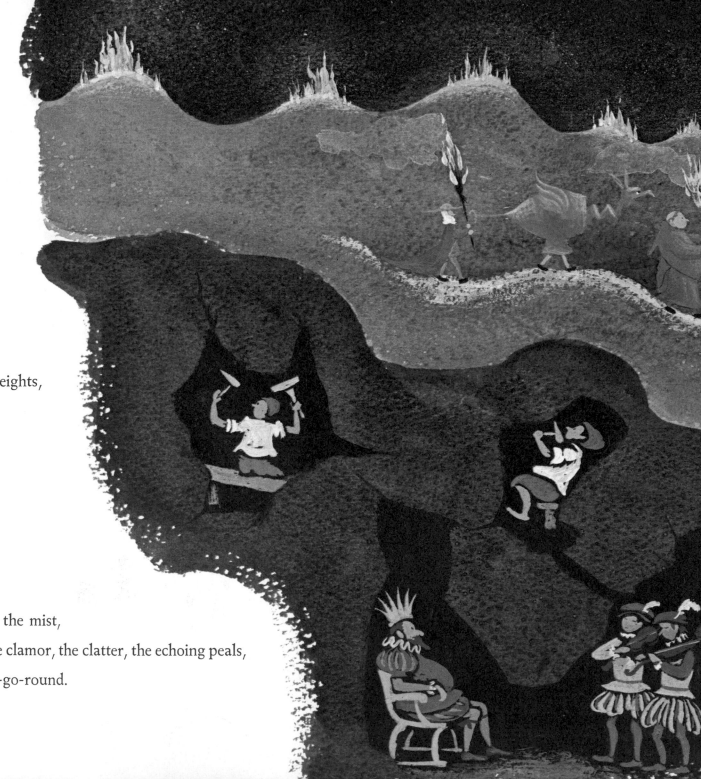

White-mitered, like bishops,
White-sheeted,
    The guisers go out,
    March round about,
        Sunwise, round about,
        Sing at each house,
                For luck,
                For cakes.

                        For this night
                        Comes Christmas in.

December 25

Before day-dawn
When the torches are out,
The hill-fires damped,
   In the dark before dawn,
   The Christmas Bull comes,

          Bellows,
          Shakes us from sleep,
          Wakes us,
               Roars at our doors,
               Till he is let in.

No one sleeps
This day of the feast.

This day all feast:

    The cattle and sheep

    In the stable and byre;

    All beasts,

    And birds.

The poor, the rich;

The fish in the sea.

      Then the Christmas folk dance,

        In the lanes,

        In the halls,

          Past fall of the night.

And feast again,

    By inches of candle,

    Cruses of grease,

    By snapping knot-light,

      Roaring hearth-light.

            For now

            Has Christmas come in.

On any, on all
The Twelve Days of Yule,
 St. George goes out,
 On a broomstick nag,
 With a wooden sword,

   And the mummers go out,
   On their nags,
   With their swords,

    After the dragon,
    After Snap.

But Snap,

Though they kill him,

Each day of the twelve,

Still lurks in the dark ways

In the back ways,

with Hobby the Horse,

and the Christmas Bull.

January 5

The season of Yule
Comes now to its end.
On the charms of this night,
Will the harvest depend.
    Light the fires about the fields,
    Drink long toasts to cow and bull,
    Pour out good ale on the apple trees,
      So there will be
          Jugs-full
          And bags-full, and
          Many baskets-full.

Twelfth Night
All the guisers of Yule,
   The mummers, go out.

The Christmas folk
Dance,
Sing merry,
And feast, on meat and on fowl.
   And he whose slice
   Of the Twelfth Night Cake
   Has the bean

                Is King of the Revels
                Carnival King.
And she
Is his queen
Who has in her slice
The dry and the hard, the lucky pea.

Yule's come and Yule's gane,
And all have feasted weel,
So Jock takes up his flail agane,
And Jenny spins her wheel.

ABOUT THE AUTHOR: Assistant professor of history at the University of Illinois, Natalia Belting is a well-known author on our Holt list, with eight successful books to her credit. Miss Belting graduated from the University of Illinois, from which she also received her Masters and Ph.D degrees. Her interest in historical research has given her the background information for each of her folklore interpretations. Along with her teaching and writing, Miss Belting finds time for her various hobbies, which include gardening, cooking, and excavating ancient artifacts of the Illinois Indians from her own property in Urbana, Illinois.

ABOUT THE ARTIST: Illustrator of over sixty books and winner of the 1958 Caldecott Medal, artist Barbara Cooney grew up in Brooklyn, New York, and attended Briarcliff School, Smith College, and the Art Students League. Varying her technique to suit each particular text, she exhibits an eye for detail few others can top. She and her husband and young children live in Pepperell, Massachusetts, in a rambling early nineteenth-century house, surrounded by broad lawns, tall trees, and lovely gardens.

ABOUT THE BOOK: Using acrylic paints in full-color illustrations, artist Barbara Cooney gives a rich, detailed interpretation to these otherwise little-known Yuletide customs. The text type is set in Weiss Roman and the display type is hand-lettered by the artist. The book is printed by offset.